Asombrosos animalitos

ESCARABAJOS

Bray Jacobson
Traducido por Diana Osorio

Gareth Stevens
PUBLISHING

Please visit our website, www.garethstevens.com. For a free color catalog of all our high-quality books, call toll free 1-800-542-2595 or fax 1-877-542-2596.

Library of Congress Cataloging-in-Publication Data
Names: Jacobson, Bray, author.
Title: Escarabajos / Bray Jacobson.
Description: New York : Gareth Stevens Publishing, [2022] | Asombrosos animalitos | Includes index.
Identifiers: LCCN 2020006185 | ISBN 9781538269091 (paperback) | ISBN 9781538269107 (6 Pack) | ISBN 9781538269114 (library binding) | ISBN 9781538269121 (ebook)
Subjects: LCSH: Beetles–Juvenile literature.
Classification: LCC QL576.2 .J34 2022 | DDC 595.76–dc23
LC record available at https://lccn.loc.gov/2020006185

First Edition

Published in 2022 by
Gareth Stevens Publishing
111 East 14th Street, Suite 349
New York, NY 10003

Translator: Diana Osorio
Editor, Spanish: Rossana Zúñiga
Designer: Katelyn E. Reynolds

Photo credits: Cover, p. 1 arlindo71/ E+ / Getty Images Plus; p. 5 Jake Jung/Moment/Getty Images; p. 7 phototrip/ iStock / Getty Images Plus; pp. 9, 24 (wings) Savas Sener/ 500px Prime/Getty Images; p. 11 Paul Starosta/Stone/Getty Images; pp. 13, 24 (eggs and grub) Christiana Fletcher/ iStock / Getty Images Plus; p. 15 YinYang/E+/Getty Images; p 17 mikroman6/Moment Open/Getty Images; p. 19 sandra standbridge/ Moment/Getty Images; p. 21 Siegfried Grassegger/Getty Images; p. 23 Gail Shumway/ Photographer's Choice / Getty Images Plus.

Printed in the United States of America

Some of the images in this book illustrate individuals who are models. The depictions do not imply actual situations or events.

CPSIA compliance information: Batch #CSGS22: For further information contact Gareth Stevens, New York, New York at 1-800-542-2595.

Find us on

Contenido

Los escarabajos viven en todos lados del mundo.

5

Existen muchos tipos.
Pueden vivir en la tierra
o en el agua.

Todos tienen seis patas.
La mayoría tiene alas.

No todos vuelan.

Ponen huevos.
Los bebés son larvas.
Sus cuerpos crecen
y cambian.

La mayoría
come plantas.

¡Las mariquitas comen otros insectos!

Pueden ser pestes.
¡Pueden acabar
con plantas!

Muchos tipos salen
de noche.

¡Las luciérnagas brillan!
Viven en lugares
cálidos.